Archipelago

Selected Works

Archipelago is dedicated to the memory of my dearest friend and fellow creative, Bruce F Press (1963-2023).

"...There you go, man
Keep as cool as you can
Face piles of trials with smiles
It riles them to believe
That you perceive
The web they weave...
And keep on thinking free"
  — Graeme Edge, *In the Beginning*
   On the Threshold of a Dream, The Moody Blues

"He had a third martini. He looked at me intently and took hold of my arm. 'Look', he said. 'You're a fish in a pond. It's drying up. You have to mutate into an amphibian, but someone keeps hanging on to you and telling you to stay in the pond, everything's going to be all right.'"
  — Jack Kerouac, *And the Hippos Were Boiled in*
   Their Tanks

"It would be absurd if we did not understand both angels and devils, since we invented them."
  — John Steinbeck, *East of Eden*

Archipelago

Selected Works

James Gossard

ARCHIPELAGO, SELECTED WORKS. Copyright © 2024 by James L Gossard. All rights reserved. No part of this book may be reproduced in any form or by any electronic or mechanical means, including information storage and retrieval systems, without permission in writing from the author, except by a reviewer, who may quote brief passages in a review. Scanning, uploading, and/or electronic distribution of this book or the facilitation of such without permission of the author is prohibited. Please purchase only authorized electronic editions, and do not participate in or encourage electronic piracy of copyrighted materials. Your support of the author's rights is appreciated. Any member of educational institutions wishing to photocopy part or all of the work for classroom use, or anthology, should send inquiries to goslit9@gmail.com.

The poem "*Erase, Texas*" © 2017 and the mini-epic poem, "*Pacific Theater*" © 2017, received the highest award for Poetry—Maryland State Arts Council Individual Artist Award in 2017. Both have been edited and updated for this publication.

This book and the stories herein are a work of fiction. Any resemblance between these fictional characters and actual persons, living or dead, is purely coincidental.

FIRST EDITION

Printed in the United States of America

First James Gossard softcover edition: November 2024

ISBN: 979-8-218-52812-6

Book Design by Ann Gossard
Cover Photograph, "Wades Point," by James L Gossard

Contents

Foreword   i

Short Stories
       The Magician   2
       The Falling Tower   11

Poetry
       Americana Truth #1   21
       Indian Summer   22
       Rage   24
       Reagan Killed Billy   26
       Americana Truth #2   28
       Erase, Texas   30
       Dead Hippies   31
       TAROT - Element 1   32
       Archipelago   33
       Construction   34
       Fences   35
       Feral   36
       Christmas   37

Stage Plays
       Book   39
       Epitaph (for Stage)   66

Screenplay
       Epitaph (for Screen)   82

Mini-Epic Poem
       Pacific Theater   98

Acknowledgements

Foreword

"How many of you are here because you actually like to write?"

The pause is deafening in this elective high school classroom. After a moment, only two hands go up.

Twenty years later, the same teacher asked the owners of those two hands to write the foreword to this book.

When we met James Gossard, he stood tall (still does), almost always in a tucked-in, button-down checkered shirt. He studied our adolescent writing efforts behind circle-framed glasses and took his role in our development seriously. We pictured him searching for the truth in our stories, which we admittedly had hidden behind clunky phrasing and the kind of writing acumen that comes with lack of experience.

A storyteller first, no matter the form, Jim's constructive criticism was expertly weighed and measured. The public-school universe worships standardized testing, and our creative work had never seen such attention before his class. It was water in the desert for us. Sam nabbed him as a mentor, and Gabe later as a screenwriting partner.

Jim's first steps after escaping home at eighteen were to run a coffee shop, raise a pig, and join a hippie commune in the San Francisco Mission District in the '70s. He became a fervent Montana outdoorsman. His work assisting biologists sent him into the frontier, where grizzly breath pushed through thin tent walls and the rising sun revealed mountain lion prints in the night's snow. Jim never really shed that face.

Somewhere in his time as a family man, he found time to run a security contract for the U.N., teach science in a strictly Orthodox school (as an atheist), and most recently, film a feature documentary about an artistic recluse. Jim' identity is an evolving kaleidoscope of lives fully lived. Savors every adventure, but ultimately—*naturally*—not yesterday's. Every new muse has found a willing servant.

And all of this curiosity, from the stories we know to the stories we are still discovering, is reflected in his works. Because Jim Gossard has lived. More than you, more than us. The tales in *Archipelago* span the full thematic breadth of the United States since the 1950s—polished and made ever more meaningful by his mastery of multiple mediums, from being an award-winning playwright and poet to a writer of screenplays and prose, as well as the producer and director of the aforementioned documentary, *Divine Instinct*, which as of this writing has no fewer than seventeen film festival laurels on the poster.

Seemingly limitless passion drives Jim from project to project, and that has birthed technique. You should listen to him speak in the following pages. He's got things to say, and excitingly and sadly, depending on the subject, they are as relevant as ever, whether you're reading something he wrote a year ago or a piece he began forty years ago to deliver now.

Jim is every one of us who decided that obsession's ride was worth the cost of admission. Of the many things we've learned from Jim, one standout is that it's okay—even beautiful—to let go of the controls and let the story take over. Ravenous curiosity is a gift and curse for the author. The writing projects tend to consume. Everything else falls away until there is only *the story*. Inspiration strikes and Jim swerves off the road (literally, that's not hyperbole, he did this) to jot down character notes. He locks himself in his tower and hammers forging fingers against anvil keys while his neighbors sleep. And he'll wake before dawn to fire up the furnaces again.

Listen up. Jim's talking. Class is in session. If the trope "write what you know" has any truth, then you should turn the page. Among anyone, Jim *knows*.

Gabe Fremuth
Graphic Novelist and Screenwriter

Sam LeGrys
Emmy Award-winning Producer

Short Stories

The Magician

Nineteen-year-old Virgil slouched on the worn clapboard porch pushing his thumbnail in the dry rot between white paint cracks on the railing. The Kansas City summer reminded him of August in North Carolina.

"This is the devil's heat," he muttered to the stifling air—something his grandmother always said.

He surveyed the long steps of the crumbly and faded Victorian house, now two apartments. Nina had gone before him stepping into the foyer. She rapped on the first-floor apartment. A slight breeze kicked through Virgil's hair, heating the sweat that edged his forehead. Virgil's job—find the baby.

The door opened a crack.

* * *

Nina had picked up Virgil at the church where he lived.
"It's a long-pants day," she said.
Virgil preferred his cutoff blue jeans. They were a second skin. Coming from Nina, the comment didn't feel like a put-down—after all, he was just a skinny kid.
"Okay," he said at last, shrugging.
Virgil trudged back inside, through the rectory to the narrow stairway that led to his tiny room. He tossed the cutoffs on the bed and slipped into rumpled khakis. The t-shirt might not be appropriate, either, so he pulled on a dark-blue shirt with small green polka dots, leaving it unbuttoned. He had found both articles of clothing in the church's cellar rooms, filled with middle-class discards and surplus foods for the poor. The remaining city churches tried to keep stocks for the needy.
In the car, Nina continued to instruct Virgil, her New England accent out of place in the declining Missouri city. Just twenty-four, she had permanent wrinkles and dark eyes.
"This is just what happens," she said. "We do all this shit for them." She pronounced it she-it.
"We get them settled, and they fuck it up. It's not like they mean to—they just do. You have to act like everything is normal. You can't let them sense you think they are anything but normal."
"I can handle it," Virgil said.
He fidgeted in his seat.

* * *

Nina held the knob firm in her hand.
"Remember what you need to do," she said.
Virgil shifted his gaze downward, unsure if he agreed.

Inside the dark apartment, Nina glided, spectral-like, and gestured to the kitchen where the three of them took seats around a red table with rust-spotted, chrome legs. The woman had the bearing of a clumsy Santa Claus, fat, but more jowly. Fat as Virgil's Aunt Carrie, the one his father called Aunt Scary.

"Coffee?" The woman's voice sounded like a diesel truck rolling over gravel. She lumbered to her feet. Her food came from the church pantry, including the shiny gallon can of government peanut butter, left open, a smear of its hydrogenated contents across the counter.

"Sure," Virgil said. He watched a roach escape from under the mug and skitter across the counter. Too late for him, but Nina said, "No."

The woman had sallow eyes. Her breasts, which had fascinated him months earlier, no longer interested him. Virgil had forgotten her name.

"How have you been, Marie?" Nina asked. She knew them all.

Under the table, Nina placed her foot on top of Virgil's foot and pressed down.

"I'm good. We're all good," Marie said.

"Where is everyone?" Nina asked.

"Bobby, he's gone to Oklahoma to find work, and Emily's over her friend's and all."

"What about Bobby Junior?"

Nina pushed on Virgil's foot again, and this time he got up and walked into the living room to hunt for Bobby Junior. The place smelled faintly like shit and a lot like piss. Nina and the woman didn't seem to mind.

"I hear they tore down your church," Marie said.

Virgil allowed their conversation to drift into background noise. There had been a baby. There had been a baby and a little girl and a husband and Marie. Virgil circled the room. The living room television perched precariously on a ratty cart showing more rust. "The Price is Right." Spin the fucking wheel, Bob. The wheel clicked, passed one dollar, fifteen cents, and stopped on eighty cents.

He stepped into an adjacent bedroom. An accumulation of clothes on the bed created an outline similar to a dead body at a crime scene. Virgil's mother always made him fold the laundry.

Sunlight filtered through tall windows, filthy except where they were open. A smaller television, surrounded by expired cosmetics, sat on a vanity. Behind it, the mirror gave off a gray film that made it unusable. The television crackled with audience applause.

Nothing under the bed—nothing in the closet.

Virgil entered the only other bedroom. Empty crib slatted sides askew. The smell of shit stronger in this room. A twin mattress lay on the floor. Blankets were heaped on stained sheets. But there, folded neatly and placed on the edge of the mattress, lay the blue dress, neatly-folded.

* * *

Nina and Virgil lounged in the dark Methodist parish house, a few miles from Virgil's Presbyterian church. A few bare light bulbs threw shadows, but neither seemed to care about the resulting edges of darkness. Nina played guitar, and they sang Kingston Trio folk songs since none of them had a television. Nina lived here.

They sat crossed-legged, as if a summer campfire burned between them. A window air conditioner cranked on, grunting a losing battle against the summer Midwest air. Condensate dripped monotonously to the floor, where it pooled, buckling the thin strips of gray-painted oak.

Nina stopped strumming and put the guitar down. She walked behind Virgil and massaged his neck.

"They're demolishing the church next month," Nina said.

Soothed by Nina's touch and mesmerized by the orange lamplight reflecting through the stained-glass transom over the front door, Virgil murmured, "What church"?

Nina and Virgil showed movies all summer outdoors at the Methodist church. Old Three Stooges flicks played against the hot depression of the inner city. They popped popcorn and fed the street bums. Here, too, Virgil taught the children to draw and write poetry.

"They're going to auction the furnishings and architectural features. Then they're going to make it a parking lot," Nina said.

The doorbell rang. Virgil opened one of the double doors, and a family stood there. He ushered them in.

The man pressed his ball cap to his gut. His wife, an enormous woman, maneuvered him in with one outstretched arm, the other holding a child.

A timid girl in a bright red dress that choked her at the neck followed. She grasped her mother's skirt hem, and they shuffled a few steps forward.

"We're Methodist," the man said. "We were told we could come here."

Virgil stared at the woman's breasts. They hung heavy, like cantaloupes in a sling. He couldn't remember ever seeing any like this. Here before him, a scarecrow-stick of a man stood with this woman with magnificent breasts. A vision of a fat Madonna, the world revolved around her, with the little girl seizing her dress and the baby Jesus, in her arms. Nina came behind Virgil and cuffed the back of his head. The man twisted his cap in his hands and stared at the floor.

"It doesn't matter if you're Methodist or not," Virgil said. "You're welcome here, and we'll do what we can."

"Take them down to the food-and-clothing lockers in the basement," Nina said. "Get them what they need. I'll call and find a place for them to stay for a few days."

They did this all the time—Nina and Virgil—serving dispossessed, wandering families.

"C'mon," Virgil said, leading them to a narrow stairway that the woman had to navigate sideways. At the bottom of the stairs, Virgil pulled out the key and smiled, holding it up for them to see. He opened the door on the middle-class treasures left behind by the white population that fled to newly minted suburbs.

Racks of clothing seemed to go on for miles. Virgil pushed past moldy fur coats.

"I need a fifty-two double D bra or bigger." The woman, courageously frank, continued. "They're not an easy size to find. I'm a big woman."

"Yeah, uh, this way," Virgil said.

On the way to the bra table, Virgil stopped and shoved his hands through clothing packed tight on the racks. He snagged a blue dress for the little girl. When he held it against her for size, she stood motionless, her lips tight together.

"Don't be impolite," her mother said, slapping her cheek. "Your dress is fine."

But the soiled, red dress was tight, like the girl had awakened in it after growing several sizes.

"No, it's okay, really. We have lots." He tried to stare down the mother but averted his eyes first.

Virgil handed the child the blue dress with white lace. She clutched it like a rag doll, eyes still dull.

Virgil had never paid much attention to this part of the room. Paint peeled from the walls, and water-stained pipes crisscrossed the ceiling, dripping stalactites of asbestos. The table they approached had a spaghetti pile of bras on it.

The woman smiled when Virgil found her size. Virgil, the Magician. They were timid picking through more clothing—apologetic, hungry. Virgil offered up leopard leotards and a housecoat dotted with daisies that he imagined might fit the woman. They could take what they needed. He led them to the pantry, and they filled boxes with food.

Upstairs, Nina had made calls and found them lodging and even had a lead for a part-time janitorial job for the man. When they left, the young girl trailed the family out with the blue dress tucked under her arm.

* * *

After checking the closet and bathroom, Virgil returned to the living room. The woman sat with her back to him. Virgil cocked his head, trying unsuccessfully to get Nina's attention.

The woman lit cigarette after cigarette. She lit one when one already burned in the ashtray. Had they not been Tareyton, Virgil would have tried to bum one.

He wanted to leave. No baby—just two televisions, stained mattresses, a rickety crib, and the blue dress.

Scratching. Virgil bit his tongue and tasted blood-iron. Scratching.

* * *

Virgil had never seen a wrecking ball in real life. It hung rusted and loose on a derrick. The crane and the orb appeared small next to the massive church and the parish house.

The man in the rig pulled at long levers and the whole machine swiveled, causing the huge iron ball to swing in a slight arc. It moved slowly, building an odd momentum. It touched the building at first, scratching off brick with a smattering of red chips. But on the next swing the weight of the machine bit deep. The man idly let the machine do the work, swing after swing.

At the first real smash, the oxygen left the universe and the crowd gasped. When the sanctuary crumbled, a turret-like tower, with spiral stairs to the balcony, crashed down. It exploded across a hole where the pulpit once stood. Virgil held his hands over his ears.

Brick dust roiled into the air and took a long time to settle, choking those too close. After the wrecking ball stilled, a bulldozer chewed at the twisted jumble. The place, where people had once come together, collapsed in on itself, reduced to construction debris. Virgil rubbed at his eye. Nina touched his arm. All of the rituals disappeared in the debris.

* * *

Virgil moved toward the scratching. The sound came from inside the sofa. Virgil grimaced at a large, wet splotch on one of its lemon-lime flowered cushions. The scuffing sound grew louder, and he touched the sofa.

He had to. Half-lifting, half-hauling, Virgil strained, pulling the overstuffed sofa diagonally from the wall.

The living being clutched a white and brown mass.

"Nina?" Virgil's voice sounded large in his head, but only a rasping noise emerged.

"Nina."

Virgil slid the couch out more, and a golem stared up with bulging eyes. He or she, it was hard to say, had crawled into the cavernous space between wall and couch, searching for food or a safe place to eat. Rewarded, legs crossed with two hands gripping a wadded peanut butter sandwich, the baby sat.

Bile seared the back of Virgil's throat. He swallowed forcefully, so it didn't spray onto this tiny person. It burned hard going back down.

Never having held a baby before, Virgil still thought he knew the rules. But this was too much. The mother lit another smoke in her kitchen.

Virgil lifted the child—oh god, don't let the yellow, brown diaper thing fall off. Act like everything is normal.

* * *

Autumn beat the summer heat into a memory, and the city air felt fresh. Virgil sat in the Presbyterian office eating onion rings, drinking Dr Pepper. He heard the door scrape open and got up to check. A small family stood in the vestibule. He recognized them immediately—Marie, Emily, and Bobby.

Bobby pressed his hat tight into his stomach. Marie pushed him forward. Emily, in her stained blue dress with white lace, followed. Her eyes shifted dully, and Virgil saw the despair and the suffering.

"We're Presbyterians," the man began, and faltered. "We've been Presbyterians our whole life."

Virgil acted like he didn't notice their revamped story. He smiled in his practiced way and took them to the cold cellar where the Methodist bras had turned Presbyterian and waited in a pile of spaghetti snakes.

"Yeah, I know, fifty-two double D or bigger."

They looked frightened.

"It's okay, I'll find what you need, I'm the Magician."

The Falling Tower

Bobby Tide lay quiet while Jack moved off the mat to peer through a crack in the wall.

"I thought the pain would be worse," Bobby said.

"Bloody hell. I don't know how one measures 'worse' in this place."

"Have they brought us any food?"

"Nothing for three days—but at least we haven't been beaten. No sign of our friend, Dungface."

"Just stay with me, Jack. I'm sorry for the smell. I know it stinks."

Neither man had seen the sky since being brought to the camp, somewhere in the damp earth jungles of Cambodia. The men, one from America and the other from Australia, lived in shadows. They shared the only mat in one corner of a squalid cell. Skinny rats circled the bo, the toilet bucket the men used. A sole rat sat on its haunches over one of their empty food bowls.

"They're there all the time, now. I think they know."

"Don't speak that way," Jack said.

"It's easier for me if I talk about it."

"We need to be prepared for the helicopters. When they come for us, they'll drop from the sky like hell's fury on these fucking ants."

"Talk to me, Jack. I love hearing your accent," Bobby said.

"Oh right, Bobby, like when they first tossed you in here, and you said I was from bloody England."

"You straightened me out on that, O'Halloran, 'I'm from Perth, mate.'"

Bobby grimaced stretching his cramped leg.

"What a mimic! You're better than when they brought you here and you started carving imaginary statues. Remember all that moving around, maneuvering between your make-believe works in marble? A bit daft—screaming at me when I walked through them."

"I wish I had a cold one," Bobby said.

He had known his time was up when Jack rolled him over to help him pee. Jack had to pull Bobby's pajama bottoms down and hold his cock while finagling the bo sideways so Bobby could relieve himself. The darkened pee dribbled on his thigh, and he managed to touch it and smell the thickness before Jack could wipe it away.

Bobby knew he'd never have a chance to finish the things he'd started—never repair the damage of his fucked-up relationships.

This was the way it would end—craving a cold one.

* * *

Tom stomped off the porch. He climbed into the only car, a VW Bug, slamming the door on his heel. He cursed, pulled the door half-shut and drove away, leaving his wife with

Bobby. Irene stood next to Bobby on the porch that wrapped around three sides of the white clapboard house, its tattered shutters closed to protect the windows from Kansas tornados. She wiped her hands on the flowered apron.

Irene shrugged and took Bobby to the kitchen. Side-by-side, barefoot, at the maple drop-leaf table, Irene taught him the mystery of bread-making and yeast. The dough they were kneading raised white dust off the board, covering their arms and aprons in its mist. He liked having his hands in the warmth, working over the table, letting his shoulder brush against hers.

While the dough rose in the bread pans, he fetched shoes and they strolled outside to her garden. Seven-foot-tall tomato plants ripe with fruit, sprawls of squash and cucumbers, pole beans and vegetables he'd never heard of, like kohlrabi, massed in her country backyard. She let him walk close to her.

After dinner they sat on the porch swing, a big open space between them filled with the recent memory of Tom. She told him that he could sleep on the couch and that she would give him a ride home in the morning.

At 3 a.m. Bobby gave up on sleeping and walked onto the porch. Tom had not returned. He wandered back into the house and stood outside Irene's door. He let his hand touch a wood panel. Maybe he meant to push the door. Because it creaked open about a foot.

Irene called out for Tom. Bobby could only say, no, it's me.

She asked if he was okay, and he said it was cold. He stepped over the threshold, letting the door move against his shoulder. In the shadows without hesitation, she lifted her covers.

This was his first time with a woman. He slipped into the room and into her bed.

Her scent was new, like spring daffodils, and his hands shook as he fumbled with her pajama top. When it fell away, he touched her breasts. Irene unsnapped his pants and pushed them down around his ankles. She guided him into her, pushing her hips into his.

In the morning, they found Tom face down on the couch, one arm under his head, the other stretched across the floor. They left him, and when they reached Bobby's home, he wanted her to come up with him, but she told him she was going away. He pleaded with her to let him come, but she said, "No, I have to do this alone." She left him standing, watching the backend of the VW as it disappeared down the road.

* * *

"Will you take me around Australia when I come to visit?"

"Sure, we'll go into the outback and dance with all the Sheilas in Melbourne."

"Yeah, I'm every bit the man for them. Why would you bring up women, here? You shit."

"Oh, don't go getting holy on me, Bobby. I hear you in your sleep."

"They told us not to jerk off."

"You do it in your sleep. At least you used to."

"We're all we have now," Bobby said. "Everything else has fallen, like the Tower of Babel."

They came for Bobby after that, even though he could no longer walk. Two boys half-carried, half-dragged him, while a third followed with a bayoneted rifle.

In another chamber, they removed his pajamas and dropped him on the stool in the center of the room. The two boys held him up while others streamed in bringing ropes that they lashed around his wrists. They fed the rope ends into metal hoops anchored on either side of the room and together the boys hauled him up, like sailors hoisting the mainsail, dislocating his shoulders when his feet lurched off the ground.

Bobby cried for Irene when his arms separated from their sockets.

The master turnkey, Dungface, squeezed Bobby's jaw and yanked his face until they were close enough for Bobby to smell rotten fish. He slapped Bobby's cheek and began instructing the boys. Each carried a stick of bamboo. Dungface used his to snap Bobby's balls. Bobby screamed.

Bobby tried to confess, agreed to sign papers, to do anything, be anything, if only they would stop. Dungface grabbed his ankle, lifting it like balsa wood, pointed to various places on the bottom of the foot. He had his disciples strike their bamboo across each spot.

When they dropped Bobby inside the cell, Jack pulled him to the mat. He cradled him in his arms with nothing else to offer.

* * *

Jack snored softly, curled up alongside Bobby. His arm stretched over him. Bobby lay awake, feverish—swelling nausea racked him, and he retched and vomited. But there was nothing, not even water in his stomach. Jack stirred and rubbed Bobby's neck.

"It's okay," Jack whispered.

But Bobby knew it wasn't and after a while could not feel Jack's touch, just the pressure of a presence on his chest, which made each breath harder to suck in than the last.

* * *

He knew Christopher before he met Irene. Christopher had gotten the acid and they were in a country dump, rolling giant tires off a cliff into a river below. The acid, "Owsley," Christopher had said. Bobby didn't know what that meant.

"It's Owsley acid, White Lightning. We're going to trip. You said you wanted to and I got some. Owsley's, like, the giver of this stuff. His is perfectly pure."

Bobby thought it looked too small to be anything, so he swallowed it.

"Yeah, we're both virgins, man," Christopher said. "This is it."

After a while, the valley below rippled and he could feel the energy intensify in his groin. Then the colors shifted and he realized that reality wasn't constant. At least not constant like he'd believed. When he looked Christopher in the face, he felt intense love and reached up to touch an aura that surrounded him. The air seemed to spark when his hand touched the edge of that pulsing light. Christopher took his hand and pressed it inside his shirt on his bare chest. Bobby felt the heart beat and closed his eyes.

They stayed up all night until the hallucinations ebbed and then Christopher took Bobby to the shower and undressed him. The magic in the acid rush returned in the adrenaline of love making. He'd never spoken about Christopher to anyone.

* * *

"How do you feel this morning?" Jack asked.

Bobby blinked while Jack wiped the crust from his eyes.

"Do you think you can eat? They brought a bowl of soup with some rice and maybe some vegetables in it."

"I'd rather have that beer you promised."

"Well, if you drink some broth, I might let you have the beer. The broth will make you strong—the beer, not so much."

So this is how you die—arguing over a fucking imaginary beer—having it held hostage until you take your medicine or eat your gruel. This is it, the great ending with the one you love.

"I was born on September 14, 1950. That made me number one. I drew number one in the lottery. That's fucked up. I was going to be a preacher," Bobby said.

Jack nodded. He brought the food to the mat and squatted beside Bobby, helping him sit up. Jack supported him and lifted the bowl to his lips. Bobby tried to sip around the bugs and rat feces. Meanwhile, Jack kicked at the rats that came for the food.

"I think it would be all right, if you just talked and let me hear your accent. Tell me about the Aboriginals and the Outback."

Jack put down the bowl and held Bobby.

"I'll introduce you to my mum, Sadie, and my da, Aiden. The whole family, Bobby. You'll meet them all—my sisters Zoe and Claire, brother Quinn. We'll make a party of it."

Bobby put his hand on Jack's chest. The pain seemed to have gone.

* * *

One bright spring day Bobby convinced Melanie to see a rerun of Russ Meyer's 'Vixen!' She wasn't comfortable with the idea of going to a porn movie at an underground theatre. He was nervous, because he didn't want to push a boner in public.

The theatre was a hole-in-the-wall place down an alleyway. Used, mismatched theater seats mounted on a flat floor that did not slope to the screen. He scanned the seating, seeing old men and few couples. They slipped into seats where he thought they could be alone.

Melanie nuzzled into him, her long brown hair playing down his shirt, catching on buttons.

They laughed when Vixen came on to her brother in the film. Melanie leaned over and told him that Vixen's breasts weren't real. He wondered how she could tell.

She took his hand and slid it inside her blouse. She let him push under her bra. Later Melanie sat on the edge of his bed and pulled him toward her. He thought about Christopher and Irene. When she popped the fly buttons of his bellbottoms, he was suddenly engorged.

* * *

"I want you," Bobby said.
His erection pushed against Jack, waking him.
"You what?" Jack whispered, then, "No, it's okay."
"I love you."

* * *

When Bobby woke, he saw light, like he remembered from Kansas. He heard helicopters, and he heard them rain terror on the NVA and the Cambodians who made the camp.

When the door burst open, one of his own in full combat gear scooped him up.

"We're going to get you home, buddy," the soldier said.

"I think I have the blackwater fever," Bobby said.

"We have medics waiting for you. C'mon, let's get you on board first."

Bobby looked for Jack, but he was not with him. Maybe he was just ahead.

They put him on the helicopter that had a falcon painted on the nose. Bobby loved falcons and when the helicopter swept into the air, he felt cool for the first time in years. The top of the jungle canopy gave way to the beaches. They flew out over the South China Sea toward a waiting carrier. He dreamed about the cold beer when he looked into the waves. He thought he saw a huge serpent undulate through the foam crests and rear his head up in triumph. The pressure in his chest disappeared.

* * *

Jack slept late into the day, holding Bobby in his arms. The sounds of the rats scratching had ceased, and he dreamed of himself holding a Victoria Bitter in a pub with giant ceiling fans. His wife was there, but something made her angry. Then rats poured through the doors, and he woke.

Poetry

AMERICANA TRUTH #1

It's a privilege
To grow old
In a society that
Does not revere the elder

Formaldehyde dreams
Permeate a place where
They can live
Unfettered…

Until they die
Or go broke and
Pass on to the dole

Or go screaming into
A gutter hole
To die of exposure
In one final dance

Across the concrete Floor

INDIAN SUMMER

Do you think the turtles dream?
Their quiet dread rises.
From where they sleep
Deep in concentric circles

And in their dreams.
Was there ever peace?
When the world spoke
Of trying the young as adults.

Who dares the somber robes?
Conceding the undeveloped mind?
When there is the matter –
Of stagnant pools beyond the bridge.

Along that bridge path,
This deafening absence –
Of geese, their autumn chatter.
Unsettled. In the manner of seasons.

They do not leave over their children?
To the turtles, who sleep in the manner eons prescribed.
Yet, in no time, do we find the simple cascading truth?
Death. Death. And if that is not enough. Death.

It plays the wild card, like the hips of wild rose.
Visible now for the first time.
Parlaying a simple eloquent truth.
Sacrifice the child.

Doesn't it pain you in the least?
This ease at which we abandon our children –
Those things most dear. Most treasured?
That is not - Silver or frankincense or myrrh?

Is this the little christ – The Anti-Christ?
Or do we need to sneak among the reeds,
Peering through to find the little grebes?
Diving as they do.

Children test these limits –
Don't know them. But the turtles –
They sleep
One upon the other.

And our torment grows.
When the warm breezes drop defenses.
We strip naked.
Where we can't be naked.

Like the turtles who carry the burden –
Of their homes on their back.
Like the nomads, the Gypsies.
It all comes back to the season; To the turtles.

That climb on snags and trunks.
On each other.
Soak in sun and light breezes.
Warm in the Indian Summer.

RAGE

Any 17-year-old fool
can squeeze the trigger
Pull on it
Yank on it
Put others' blood on it
And be named a messiah

By an idiot with power
In power
Eating power as the
Breakfast of Champions!

Any idiot
Any fool
And there are
Will be
Followers
More fools
More idiots

Until we can't see
What fool wags the tail

With designs of
Destruction –
Rage filled for
Their own inadequacies

That stack up against the others
But there are surely some who are good

Hitler was a good man.
A collector of Art.
A monk eating simple foods.
Living an ascetic and simple life
With idiots and fools who
Followed him
Into the
Darkest Depths

The fools
Given the voice
Of indecency
Entitlement
Depravity

REAGAN KILLED BILLY

I keep thinking of Billy
Holding my hand when I wanted to die
Haunted and un-beheld

Your fear is my worst dream
I fell into that hole where mirth
and mire can never
transcend the elements of the soul

I'm a-muck in my death
Thinking of yours and how painful
And alone
You were
When I left you as a lover.

We played music
And God did not dance with us
I closed my eyes to your songs
Awash in your lilt

We swayed together
With unfiltered Camels between our lips
Yellowed teeth
In the taste of our kisses

I didn't know how you
Would die when I left you
I didn't understand
The Reagan People, then

I'm sad to tell your stone they still live
Bringing their hate on
Choking Life
Choking Our Mother

I don't see you frail and mottled
I see you in the shine of my eye
A wistful smile

I keep thinking of you, Billy
The man I loved
And lost
And remem...ber

AMERICANA TRUTH #2

We talked about rocking chairs
When we were eighteen
Lying on the ground
Shoulder to shoulder
Counting shooting stars

It was odd to even
Conceive of rocking
Our final days away
On our porch
But we did

In a romantic way
Time was forever
We lay on
Stained sheets
Holding the years

We tried
And walked away
From the heroin
Cooked in a spoon
Shot in our veins

The day we left
Each other
I was surprised
At the urgency
Of your kisses

I wish I had stayed
And returned them
Because now I rock
On the porch
With the empty rocking chair

ERASE, TEXAS

I opened my eyes in Erase, Texas

A hobo haven, abandoned
Ghost town of the damned
Clap Boarded, Corrupt Buildings
Bereft of Soul

I needed to pee
In the middle of the night
And woke in the flood plain
By a broken gazebo

Stumbling along
A thin bead of water
Among skunk cabbage
growing in the swamp of backyards

A ghost train, white and gray
Slid on, Silent -- no rumbling
No rhythm to put me to sleep
Moving to clear the town

I want to climb the concrete stairway to the tracks
Out of the cemetery
Make the train stop
Make it return the souls of the children

Searching for gems
Eating beans from a tin pot
Touching remains
Planting my soul in the dirt

of Erase, Texas

DEAD HIPPIES

I'm going to fight you

TAROT - ELEMENT 1

On that bed with Fortune and Shredded Millions,

The cards played out
    My life and I craved
        More and more answers
            In time and without

From a City on a Bay to a City on a Bay

By the water on a hill over the bay
    Where I met my First demon
        Who'd suck my very essence from me

My childhood lost in the event of his coming not mine

And that hill moved me in sick fascination and made me want it

And I fled for the safety of the Mission
    And a bigger water on the coastal backwash
        Where I dove into water too cold for man

And escaped from the surf and found myself naked in the sand
    Holding an erection
        And God was with me and my creation
Which was lost in the cards on the bed with
    Shredded Millions
        With all the events of my life laid out
            In a stream
                Of steps

And places just waiting for me.

ARCHIPELAGO

First some good news
Then some bad
Oh yeah –
I remember when it was about who owned the dumpster
When I won and left with the
Hydraulic lift
And the old lady kept the vegetables.

Harsh winters in Montana
Where you can't pull the collar up without
Its breaking
And then it's your back breaking
With acceptance
Wanting some relief maybe, some cash …
Something to pay the bills that eat
Out your soul

Yeah, this is America
This, American Doom
In the harsh arctic
Skirting the archipelago
All left by sharks eating the fabric
And I still keep losing …
The Will
The Meaning
The Dimension

CONSTRUCTION

She had to die alone,
but it was okay.

She had to die.
Doctor Oz said
it was a reasonable
and
Doctor Phil confirmed.

She had to die
Because we're number one.

She had to die alone
Drifting to her final sleep
With only the touch
of the mechanics
around her

Ping, ping, ping, fucking ping!

She had to die
Without a hand to hold
Because we did not have masks

She had to die
Because we're MAGA.
We have plenty of
Refrigerator trucks

And backhoes
To trench

FENCES

Trapped in a world he did not understand
the cowboy looked longingly out the window
wondering where his cows were –

He remembered campfires and horse sweat
bound in the smell of saddles, coffee, and gear
wrapped in a thin wool blanket
against a sky bigger than the universe

Held against the pain, he presses the glass
wondering how he could bring his children
into focus from the world he left
so long, long ago… in a desperate move
to build a grubstake

Riding fences, riding fences, day into night
across the mountains and into the stars
he drifts and drifts to the hack of a coyote
the squall of a hawk

on the wing – on the wing
like him

FERAL

Kids run feral.
It's what they do

Run wild
Weave between corn rows
Unaware

When they find
The hidden garden
They feast
On the Farmer's watermelon

Unaware
That this was sustenance
For a poor honyocker

Who would find
Broken rinds
And half eaten flesh

In the evening
When the old
Rock on their front porches
The kids come home to roost

With glazed over eyes
They look up to their elders
Not sure
Not sure.

CHRISTMAS

And there it is
On scarified earth
The front lawn
Covered in weeds and clover
Broken branches

Left to its devices
The weeds heal the earth
In stages

A succession of changes
One of many
To heal sterile earth
And minds

Unable to think
Without God
And so, lies there

Tossed aside
A skeleton
Of branches and wire

All the tiny leaves
Fallen
Like your angels
A headstone on
That scarified lawn

Left, like so many
Other good ideas
The Christmas Wreath

Stage Plays

BOOK

A Play in One Act

Cast of Characters

Syzygy: Any age; any gender.

Voice: Clear and sure; any age; any gender.

Mephis: Pressed khaki pants; white dress shirt; 25-30 years old; any gender.

Sequoia: Living-on-the-street; worn and dirty clothing; 17-20 years old; female.

Evander: Living-on-the-street; worn and dirty clothing; 17-20 years old; male.

Scene

A sparsely furnished office in a rundown business building on the seedy side of town.

Time

The present.

ACT I

SETTING: Office with a single long table and three chairs, evenly and neatly spaced. To the side, a stool near the door. A black and white picture of a cross hangs perfectly level and prominently displayed, facing the audience.

AT RISE: SYZYGY sits on the stool, watching over the ROOM. Arms crossed.

SYZYGY
(Jumps off stool, singing, loud, A Capello.)
Ah... a... men... Hmmmm. Guh... Ah... a... men... Ah... a... men...

(SYZYGY strides with purpose to the picture and slides it on its hanger making it grotesquely out of level, before returning to the stool.)

(Footsteps from off stage, one set coming downstairs. Two sets coming upstairs)

VOICE
(off)
Sucker!

                    MEPHIS
             (off)
It's quiet in here. You'll find it peaceful.

             (Enter MEPHIS and
             SEQUOIA. Upon entering,
             SYZYGY moves behind
             MEPHIS, like a shadow.)

             (Stage lights dim. Spot on
             MEPHIS. Spot on
             SEQUOIA.)

                    SEQUOIA
Who was that out there?

                    MEPHIS
Bad seed. He's not welcome here.

                    SEQUOIA
I'm really hungry. Feeling dizzy.

             (MEPHIS takes SEQUOIA
             by the arm, patting it.)

                    MEPHIS
I know life on the street can be tough. I was there once.
You'll have more food than you can eat, soon enough. We
just need a little information. Our best way to help you
improve your situation is with this questionnaire. It's a
simple audit, if you will, so we can get you what you need.

             (SEQUOIA yanks her arms
             away and slides her hand
             along the cuff of her sleeve,

> feeling for something. She
> backs away from MEPHIS.)

SEQUOIA

Can I get a snack, please? Some water? I haven't eaten for two days.

MEPHIS

Of course. Let's get you set up, here.
> (Stage lighting returns to normal. MEPHIS guides SEQUOIA and seats her at the table. Every action by MEPHIS is deliberate and gentle, but there's no arguing with the persuasive, physical presence. At each seat is a questionnaire booklet and pencil.)

Our server's down, so we're doing it the old-fashioned way. You can start your audit while I fetch some food. You know, it's just a survey. We can serve you better this way. I'll get you some snacks and water. We'll make sure you have everything you want.

> (MEPHIS smiles and exits. SYZYGY returns to the stool.)

SEQUOIA

Thanks.

> (SEQUOIA slides a switch blade from her sleeve as she leaves the table. She flicks it open and walks around the room, touching items with the

>   point of the blade. She's
>   obviously nauseous. She
>   returns to the table and lays
>   the knife down. She lifts the
>   questionnaire booklet and
>   thumbs through it.)

                    SEQUOIA (Continued)
>   (mimicking MEPHIS)
Oh. You know, it's just a silly 'little' survey. We can serve you better this way. You wanna serve me? Just feed me.
>   (She sits and flips pages in
>   the booklet. Perusing the
>   questions, she sticks the blade
>   in the table, twisting it
>   lightly.)
What am I doing here? Stop!
>   (She closes the knife and
>   slips it up her sleeve.)
Please.

>   (She breathes deeply and
>   settles in to fill out the
>   'Answer' sheet. While she
>   fills in bubbles, SYZYGY
>   leaves the stool, goes to
>   SEQUOIA'S table, pulls out
>   a chair, spins it around, and
>   straddles it.)

                        SYZYGY
Hmmmm... Guh...

                        SEQUOIA
I can't think this way!

SYZYGY

Gar... gar... tee... Dough... nnn.... Ah... a... men... Hmmmm. Guh... Ah... a... men... Ah... a... men...

(SYZYGY takes all of SEQUOIA'S materials and moves them to the floor. Without interaction with SYZYGY, SEQUOIA follows the booklet. She moves to the floor continuing her work on the questionnaire.)

(SYZYGY picks up the chair and takes it center stage, near SEQUOIA. SYZYGY sits.)

SEQUOIA
(reading)

As it pertains to you, True or False: I have a tendency to manipulate or exploit others to achieve my own goals or desires.

(rubs her belly)

Who manipulates who? I really need food. I think I'm going to throw up.

(Fills in sheet. Reads.)

True or False: I have difficulty maintaining healthy and stable relationships due to interpersonal conflicts. Eww, and another? I have difficulty maintaining healthy and stable relationships due to trust issues. Whadda ya think? Do we have trust issues?

(fills in sheet)

I can't do this anymore. I'm hungry. So hungry.

(looks around, frantic)

SEQUOIA (Continued)

God, I need to puke. There's no trash can. I need sleep so badly.

(SEQUOIA pushes the questionnaire aside and stretches out on the floor cradling her head. Eyes close. Lights dim.)

(a long silence)

VOICE
(off)

Sucker!

MEPHIS
(off)

It's quiet in here. You'll find it peaceful.

(SEQUOIA stirs and places her hand at the cuff of her sleeve. Enter MEPHIS and EVANDER. SYZYGY stands and flips the chair upside-down then shadows MEPHIS.)

(Lights rise.)

(MEPHIS takes EVANDER by the arm, stroking it.)

EVANDER

Like I told you, I'm really hungry.

MEPHIS
Everyone is. I know life on the street can be tough. You'll have more food than you can eat, soon enough. You'll get so much food; you'll be tired of eating. We only need a little information. Our best way to help you improve your situation is with this questionnaire. It's a simple audit, if you will, so we can get you squared away.

(MEPHIS guides EVANDER and seats him at the table in the remaining chair. Every action by MEPHIS is deliberate and gentle, but there's no arguing with the persuasive, physical presence.)

EVANDER
Can I get something to eat? Some juice?

MEPHIS
Of course. Let me get you set up, here. Our server's down, so we're doing it the old-fashioned way. You start working on this, and I'll see about some food.

SEQUOIA
Hey, you promised me some food.

MEPHIS
It's coming.

(MEPHIS exits. SYZYGY returns to the stool. EVANDER studies the questionnaire.)

(EVANDER and SEQUOIA look at each other, trying not to notice each other. It's the look of wanting to know where to not look or engage.)

SEQUOIA

Well, are you going to say anything?

EVANDER

(mumbling)

Evander.

SEQUOIA

What is eva under?

EVANDER

Eva is not under anything. My name is Evander.

SEQUOIA

How did you get here?

EVANDER

I haven't eaten in days. They promised me food. Lots of food.

SEQUOIA

Same. But all I've gotten so far is this stupid personality test. Still, it's nice to be off the street.

EVANDER

Yeah. They promised me a better life.

SEQUOIA

Same. What do you think they meant by that?

                    EVANDER
Dunno. They told me I would be able to live in a safe place.

                    SEQUOIA
There's no free lunch. Got to be an easier way to get food and shelter than filling out this crap. It really sucks. Wait till you get to the questions on your erection.

                    EVANDER
You're kidding, right?

                    SEQUOIA
I don't kid.

                    EVANDER
Right.
          (lifts his book)
This whole thing?

                    SEQUOIA
Crazy.

                    (SEQUOIA and EVANDER
                    work on their audit.
                    SYZYGY leaves the stool
                    and takes EVANDER's
                    materials away from the
                    table, putting them on the
                    floor. EVANDER follows,
                    picking up on the task
                    without missing a beat.
                    SYZYGY proceeds to upend
                    the table and any remaining
                    furniture is moved to create
                    chaos and disorder around
                    SEQUOIA and EVANDER.)

                    EVANDER
What?
            (sits straight, holding up his
            booklet)
I see what you mean. True or False: I regularly
communicate openly with sexual partners about my sexual
health status.

                    SEQUOIA
Told you. Do you?

                    EVANDER
I live on the street and eat out of dumpsters. I haven't had
sex in ... I don't want to talk about it.
            (reading)
Jeez! True or False: I regularly get tested for STDs,
including HIV.

                    SEQUOIA
Tell it to your paper.

                    EVANDER
            (reading)
Have you ever struggled with mental health issues such as
depression or anxiety? Yes or no.
            (looks at SEQUOIA, who
            ignores him)
Yes, No: Have you ever had thoughts of self-harm?

            (Enter MEPHIS with two
            paper plates stacked on each
            other. There's one plain piece
            of white bread on each plate.
            SYZYGY shadows
            MEPHIS.)

SEQUOIA
It's a 'personality' test, doofus.

MEPHIS
We don't name call inside.

SEQUOIA
It's a term of endearment.

MEPHIS
Not here. It's not allowed. We are the bulwark against those out there. Against the noise.

SEQUOIA
Whoa! Those? Out there?

MEPHIS
You'll appreciate it in time. And there's plenty of time for that later. Meanwhile, I brought food. I forgot the forks, though.

(MEPHIS gives a plate to each.)

SEQUOIA
A piece of white bread? Forks? This is all the food I'll ever want? You fuck!

MEPHIS
It's humble. Yes. Be grateful. More will come after the audit. More than you can imagine.

EVANDER
You promised me juice.

MEPHIS

It'll come. Be patient. Trust me. Finish your audit, and there will be so much food that you'll not want food anymore. Like I said, you'll get tired of food.

EVANDER

Sounds wonderful.

SEQUOIA

I'll believe it when I see it.

MEPHIS

I'll be back to collect you and your audit. We'll all share a meal.

EVANDER

Don't forget my juice. Please.

MEPHIS

Of course.

(MEPHIS exits and
SYZYGY returns to the stool.
EVANDER and SEQUOIA
work in silence for a few
beats.)

EVANDER

Let's just get this audit done so we can get some food.

SEQUOIA

Forks! What an ass. What if it's drugged?

EVANDER

The bread? No fucking way. Maybe he was just being thoughtful with the forks.

SEQUOIA
What do you know about him?

EVANDER
He seems nice. Easy to be around. Successful.
> (SEQUOIA cradles her belly and cries out as she rolls into a fetal position on the floor.)

Oh my god. Are you okay?

SEQUOIA
Do I look okay? Of course, I'm not okay. I'm going to have to pee. Help me up.

> (EVANDER goes to help SEQUOIA. As he does, the knife falls to floor from her sleeve.)

EVANDER
Whoa! What's that?

SEQUOIA
I don't know you. I don't know any of you.
> (EVANDER bends to pick up the knife and SEQUOIA pushes him away. She picks up the knife, flips it open, and brandishes it at EVANDER.)

Don't ever -
> (EVANDER stumbles back.)

EVANDER
No. No. I'm sorry. I would never hurt you. I'm not like that.

SEQUOIA
What are you like, Evander?

EVANDER
I don't know. Not like that. I wouldn't take advantage.

SEQUOIA
(like a lightbulb goes off)
I recognize your voice. I remember you. No, not you. Just your voice. There were a lot of voices.
(clutches her head)
Was it you Evander?

EVANDER
No. Where?

SEQUOIA
Behind the dumpsters in the Mission. I'm sure of it. Five fucking months ago. I couldn't see any of you. But I remember your voice.

EVANDER
I don't know what you're talking about. I wasn't there.

SEQUOIA
You were part of the train.

EVANDER
No, no, no. Whatever it is, I wasn't there. You heard someone else.

SEQUOIA
Just back away. I know your voice, now. Like it was yesterday.

EVANDER

Please.

SEQUOIA

You did this to me.

EVANDER

No. Not me. Are you... Are you-

SEQUOIA

Am I... pregnant? Do you remember now?

EVANDER

It wasn't me.

SEQUOIA

But I remember you, don't I?

EVANDER

I didn't recognize you.

SEQUOIA

Was it too dark back there? You couldn't see who you were taking turns with? I remember your voice.

EVANDER
(fearfully loud)

I tried to stop them.

SEQUOIA
(quietly)

I remember now. There was one voice. I thought it would save me, but it didn't.
(lowers the knife)
They held me down. There were so many. But it was your voice that I remember.

                    EVANDER
                (less fearful)
I couldn't stop them. They beat me up. Everyone was gone
when I woke up. I just wanted to go home. This is what
they did to me.
                (opens his shirt, revealing a
                deep scar in his chest)
It still hurts.

                    SEQUOIA
Evander. I still need to pee.

                (EVANDER goes to the door
                and tries the knob. Bangs on
                the door.)

                    EVANDER
It's locked.

                    SEQUOIA
You sound surprised.

                (EVANDER slides to the
                floor holding his head.)

                    EVANDER
I'm sorry I didn't stop them.

                    SEQUOIA
You tried.

                    EVANDER
I tried. And like everything else in life that I tried, I failed.

SEQUOIA
How did you end up out there?

EVANDER
I didn't have anyone. My mom told me to shrug it off.

SEQUOIA
What about your dad?

EVANDER
Long gone. My mom had a lot of boyfriends after that. The last one...

SEQUOIA
Must have been bad for you to run away.

EVANDER
He was a long time ago.

SEQUOIA
What was it that made you run away?

EVANDER
It doesn't matter.
    (beat)
You never told me your name.

SEQUOIA
It's Sequoia.

EVANDER
What about you?

SEQUOIA
Me? I was a fentanyl posterchild. Started dating a dealer 'cause he was so hot, and I wanted to be so cool. Bob. He was the dealer. He used to cook up all kinds of shit. Heroin laced with fentanyl. Morphine. Dunno. His stuff killed a middle school kid. It got violent at home after that. Did a stint in juvie.

EVANDER
That's rough.
         (beat)
I was going to need therapy my mom said. Said it would ruin my life. And look at where I am now. Funny, huh?

SEQUOIA
Not so funny.

EVANDER
No. Not so funny, Sequoia. The last guy my mom dated…

SEQUOIA
You're safe with me.

EVANDER
He came in my room. He smelled bad and had his belt out. I only had my pajamas on and he ripped them off and beat me for upsetting my mom.

SEQUOIA
I'm so sorry.

EVANDER
That wasn't all. He did to me what those boys did to you.

SEQUOIA
Shit.
 (beat)
Thanks for trying to save me.

EVANDER
It was years ago.
 (beat)
What are we going to do?

SEQUOIA
Fill out the survey.

EVANDER
 (laughs)
Why not?
 (SEQUOIA touches
 EVANDER'S arm and they
 have a moment of closure.
 They lie on the floor together,
 and work on their surveys.
 The lights fade for a moment.
 When the lights rise, both are
 sitting cross-legged back-to-
 back.)
What is the darkest thought you've ever had? I hate short essay.

SEQUOIA
Now, they're asking about all the things we just talked about. I don't think it's safe to fill this out.

EVANDER
It's not like they can do anything with it. I've got nothing left to hide. It's like a puzzle. I've always been good at puzzles.

SEQUOIA

It's a mindfuck, Evander. We should figure out how to get out of here.

    (The door clicks and opens.
    MEPHIS enters with two
    paper cups of water on a
    tray.)

Why is the door locked?

MEPHIS

Your own safety, of course. I brought you something to drink.

SEQUOIA

What I need is to pee.

MEPHIS

I'll have one of our ladies come and get you.

SEQUOIA

I'm pretty sure I can pee by myself.

MEPHIS

Like I said. It's for your own safety. I'll have a girl come and get you.

    (MEPHIS flips up a chair and
    puts the cups on it. Exits.)

EVANDER

After this, should we, like, live together?

SEQUOIA

What? And live happily ever after? Are you paying attention to what's going on here?

EVANDER
Dunno. I was just thinking.

SEQUOIA
You want to be a dad?

EVANDER
Maybe. At least you wouldn't have to do it alone.

SEQUOIA
I'm used to being alone.

EVANDER
Sequoia is a beautiful name.

SEQUOIA
How much more do we have to do?

EVANDER
I'm nearly done. I'm on the book question.

SEQUOIA
(flips ahead in her book)
This is fucked up.

EVANDER
What part?

SEQUOIA
All of it. We got suckered. What are you most afraid of people finding out about you? Can you talk about a significant failure in your life and how it affected you? Have you ever experienced abuse or trauma? Can you describe what happened? God! Where's the book question.

EVANDER

It's the last one.

SEQUOIA
(flips to the end of her survey)

Choose which book you would ban: "1984" by George Orwell? Classic! "The Handmaid's Tale" by Margaret Atwood? "To Kill a Mockingbird"? Come on! That's a classic, too! "Beloved" by Toni Morrison? This is a bit on the nose, don't you think? The next section is movies.

EVANDER

They're not asking you to ban books. It's a... a hypothetical.

SEQUOIA

"Catcher in the Rye"?!

EVANDER

It's just a hypothetical.

SEQUOIA

I don't think so. Have you even read these? Do you see what this question is asking? They already want to know who you're having sex with!

EVANDER

It's just a hypothetical. It doesn't mean anything.

SEQUOIA

We're being hijacked! They'll be telling you who and when to screw. There's too much weirdness. Let's get out of here.

(SEQUOIA moves to the
door and tries the handle.
Locked.)

EVANDER

I'm tired of struggling. This place is safe. They're going to have a feast. He said so. We're off the street.

SEQUOIA

Come with me. Evander. You and me. We're more alike than different. C'mon.

EVANDER
(defeated)

It's all hypothetical. It doesn't mean anything. I'm just so hungry and tired of fighting.

(Enter MEPHIS, closing the
door behind him. SYZYGY
leaves the stool and brings
more disarray to the stage,
tearing the booklets and
tossing them into the air,
moving and upending
furniture. SYZYGY moves
toward the door.)

MEPHIS

What's going on?

SEQUOIA

You messed up. Locking the door. I'm leaving.

(SYZYGY grasps the door
knob. SEQUOIA takes her
answer sheet and wads it up,

>   heading for the exit. MEPHIS
>   steps in front of her.
>   SYZYGY opens the door.)

                        MEPHIS
It's not safe out there.
            (SYZYGY closes the door.)
The world is a confusing place. We're setting up a feast for you, right now. Just like I promised. You need to calm down. We'll have our feast, and you can decide after that. You and your baby.

>   (SEQUOIA gives MEPHIS
>   the finger and pushes toward
>   the exit despite MEPHIS
>   physically blocking her.)

                        SEQUOIA
How did you know about that? You're watching us? See, Evander? They're watching us.
            (EVANDER is engrossed in
            the questionnaire.)
Evander?

>   (SYZYGY opens the door.)

                        EVANDER
            (looks at SEQUOIA)
It's okay Sequoia. I'll be alright. I'm just really hungry. I'm staying. For now.

>   (SYZYGY closes the door.)

                        MEPHIS
Evander's one of us.

SEQUOIA

Fine. Then eat this…

    (SEQUOIA throws her wadded answer sheets at MEPHIS.)

…because I can eat better out of the dumpsters!

    (SEQUOIA moves toward the exit.)

Evander.

    (SYZYGY opens the door.)

MEPHIS

Evander will be redeemed. Sequoia. Come back and finish your audit. Everything will be fine. Think of your baby.

SEQUOIA
(from the doorway)

Evander. Please come with me. It's not safe, here. We can get that house. You and me. Evander, come on. Evander, please.

    (exit SEQUOIA)

EVANDER
(excited and looking up from his questionnaire)

Sequoia, I've got it! I know the answer!

    (SYZYGY closes the door.)

    (Mephis smirks and moves toward Evander.)

(BLACKOUT)
(END)

EPITAPH

A 10-Minute Play in One Act

NOTICE: This stage play deals with sensitive material. If you are in crisis, DIAL 988. The 988 Lifeline is a national network of local crisis centers that provides free and confidential emotional support to people in suicidal crisis or emotional distress 24 hours a day, 7 days a week in the United States.

Cast of Characters

Mason: Black suit, no tie; 27, could be 21; appears to be male; similar build to Oakley.

Oakley: Light gray sweats; 21, could be 27; appears to be female; similar build to Mason.

Cop: Uniformed; 40; male.

M.E.: Dressed professionally; 50; any gender. Medical Examiner.

Scene

OAKLEY's studio apartment in a restored and gentrified warehouse.

Time

The present.

ACT I

SETTING: There is a window and the only door is open. Simple furnishings. A futon-type bed. A vase of dead flowers sits on the dresser.

AT RISE: Spot on OAKLEY sitting slumped in a semi-lotus position, head bowed, DEAD. OAKLEY's long hair covers the face. Hands stretch out, palms up. A razor blade rests against the left middle finger. The right wrist exposed and dark from blood.

Next to OAKLEY'S left hand is a framed photo. In the picture a younger OAKLEY leans in to a similarly aged SKYLAR. Their arms are crossed. Expressions of mock indifference.

OAKLEY wears earbuds. A cell phone lies nearby.

Detective MASON, wearing surgical gloves, stands in the dark by OAKLEY.

MASON
(As the light comes up, MASON kneels, gently moving OAKLEY's hair

away to press gloved fingers
to OAKLEY's carotid.)

MASON (Continued)
What were you feeling when your life slipped away?
(MASON removes an ear bud
from OAKLEY's ear,
holding it near his ear. He
sets it down by the cell phone
and picks up the phone.
Tapping the screen, he
peruses it and sets it down.)
"River." Playing in a loop? Why Joni Mitchell? Why
"River"?

(MASON picks up the
picture, considers it briefly,
and places it down before
standing and stepping to the
bed to pick up a sheet of
paper.)

OAKLEY
(not moving, loud)
Isn't it obvious?

MASON
It's never obvious. Never one hundred percent.

OAKLEY
(lifts head)
I loved to dance. He loved to dance. We were nymphs. We
danced in open fields... in the woods... in the rivers...
I loved music. It beat back the voices in my head... but
sometimes it haunted me. Then the music ended.

MASON
An eternity of nothingness-

OAKLEY
(flip of the hand)
"...a brief strut upon the stage," and then an eternity of nothingness.
(MASON crosses to the dresser and touches the dead flowers. Returns to OAKLEY.)
I loved him. When he came to me that first night, I wasn't ready. He rested his head on my shoulder. I thought he just wanted to be held, but he hungered for something that brought thunder. And joy.

I thought I liked girls, but the way he was touching me felt-- eternally familiar.

Skyler made me crazy.

(OAKLEY's head drops.
COP enters.)

COP
Detective?
(MASON startles)
M.E.'s on the way. Suicide?

MASON
Sometimes, I feel like I understand it.

COP
Just another dumb kid who didn't value life.

(COP moves to the dresser, checking drawers.)

(OAKLEY's head pops up.)

MASON
Officer, move away from the dresser. This is still a crime scene.

OAKLEY
I'm actually fucking here, you know.

COP
It's a waste of air. These people are better off in the ground, anyway.

OAKLEY
YOU. DON'T. KNOW. ME.

MASON
Don't be crass. We don't know enough.

OAKLEY
Fuck you both. I loved life. And dancing. And music. …and coffee.

COP
Is there anything in the note?

MASON
Hints. There are always hints.

COP
(sarcastic)
Poor kid, right?

MASON
(to self)
There seems to be some sexual ambiguity.

COP
Ah. There it is. That's what's wrong with this country. Christ! God gives us everything we need. What's wrong with the kids these days? They've got everything they need. They have it too easy.

(MASON's attention snaps back to COP.)

OAKLEY
Why should you care? What do you know about anything? What do you know about me? Asshat! You're a fucking cliché.

Just like me, cosmic space will feed on your face. God is dead. We're all dead.

MASON
Officer. Please wait outside.

COP
I'm just saying that you only need to look between your legs to know who you are.

MASON
Bring the M.E. when they arrive.

(COP exits in a bit of a huff.)

OAKLEY
M.E.? What do we need the Medical Examiner for?
(beat)
M.E... Me.

MASON
Was this really a suicide?

OAKLEY
Duh!

MASON
Good looking kid.

OAKLEY
I've been told.

MASON
(reading note)
"Dear Skylar." Not, "Dear World." Is this murder? Nah.

OAKLEY
I miss Skylar. I haven't seen him since he left me. It seems an eternity of aching. I only have the picture now. I can't remember his smell, his touch. It's just a fantasy now. We won't meet on some greater plane of existence. Will we?

MASON
(Picks up the photograph.)
Is this your Skylar?

OAKLEY
Of course it's him. He loved me for who I am. For a while anyway.

MASON
Was it that hard?

OAKLEY
Harder than you can imagine.

MASON
To not know who you are? To not be allowed to be who you are?

OAKLEY
Maybe it was love through suffering. Or maybe just living through suffering and the love was secondary. Why do words fail me? No one heard me when I cried. No one in the angelic orders. No one from the court of God. Skylar stopped pressing me against his heart.

MASON
Just this picture, and a lonely cry in a note to Skylar.

OAKLEY
Is that all it is, detective? Just a greater angel making time stand still in a moment that I thought was forbidden. My time with time has passed.

MASON
Why is your entire existence reduced to this picture and a lonely cry in a note to someone named, Skylar?

OAKLEY
Skylar was my biggest regret, because I fell in love with him. Oh, he made me laugh so hard that I peed myself. Our moment... our moment...

MASON
You're gay?

OAKLEY
(exasperated sigh)
I'm ambiguous. This is my interpreted world... my requiem... I'm gone now.

MASON
But it really doesn't matter anymore, because you're dead.

OAKLEY
You all are.
(beat)
Will I smell like the wet autumn leaves, rotting on the ground?

(lights fade to twilight)

MASON
(In the stage twilight,
MASON places the picture
next to OAKLEY and kneels
to pull and tie OAKLEY's
hair into a pony tail.)
I'm so sorry. "...a brief strut upon the stage," and then an eternity of nothingness.

(While lights strobe or
similar effect, OAKLEY and
MASON stand and the two
exchange their clothing with
each other.)

COP
(off)
This way. The detective's waiting for you.

                    M.E.
          (off)
I can find my way.

                    COP
          (off)
Nothing for me to do out here, and she's kinda dodgy. If you catch my meaning.

                    M.E.
          (off)
I'm sure I'll be able to sort it all out.

                    COP
          (off)
Sure. Whatever.
          (Strobe effect stops.)

          (MASON and OAKLEY wear each other's clothing. MASON no longer wears the surgical gloves. OAKLEY wears them.)

          (OAKLEY lowers MASON into the semi-lotus position where OAKLEY previously sat.)

          (Enter M.E., wearing surgical gloves, carrying a camera and small supply case. COP follows M.E. and stands looking out of the window.)

(OAKLEY puts the ear bud
in MASON's ear and stands
to face--)

M.E.

What do you have, detective?
(With deft efficiency, M.E.
photographs the different
angles of the body. The razor.
The phone.)

OAKLEY

Apparent suicide. Unrequited love. Trans identity issues.
Take your pick—another lost soul. Left a note.

M.E.

All in the note?

OAKLEY

Mostly.

M.E.

Ambiguity can be painful, I'm sure. Interesting. If you look
along his arm, you can see where he's a cutter. Suicide is
rarely the motive behind cutting. The cause of death is a
different kind of cut.
(M.E. bags the razor and the
phone. He scans the note.)
From the wound, not a murder, I'm sure. Skylar?

OAKLEY

(picks up the photo)
I believe they're together in this picture. I'll have to run
him down, but I don't think it will lead anywhere. Just
unrequited love.

                    (hands the photo to the M.E.)

                              M.E.
Idyllic. Like a place that I'd want to be. Pictures are worth a thousand words.

                              OAKLEY
Pictures can be deceiving.

                              MASON
It feels… familiar.

                              COP
D.B.'s ride is here. Are you ready to bag 'em?

                    (M.E. bags the photo, placing
                    it in his box.)

                              M.E.
In a moment.
                    (to OAKLEY)
Help me stretch him flat. Any family?
                    (Oakley and Medical
                    Examiner pull Mason from
                    his lotus position, stretching
                    him prone.)

                              OAKLEY
None so far.

                              M.E.
                    (lifts the waist band of the
                    sweats to confirm)
May be Trans, but the organs are male.

COP
What'd I tell you, detective. Just check between the legs.

M.E.   OAKLEY
Take it outside.   Take it outside.

M.E.
Have them bring in the gurney.

COP
I'll send 'em up. You can escort the body out; I'm going off shift.

(exit COP)

MASON
Not even one final plea? It's strange. No longer inhabiting the earth. I felt the world inside me just then.
(M.E. collects his gear and
exit.)

OAKLEY
(looking down on Mason)
Skylar? Do you remember the time that you climbed into a huge hollowed out tree stump?
(Strobing effect begins.
OAKLEY kneels and lifts
MASON)
You were in all of your glory. You told me that you'd never done it in a tree before.
(MASON and OAKLEY
exchange clothing.)
I remember melding into that soft, moist earth. With you. Into you. The millipedes fled from our embrace. We played in a world of worlds.

(MASON lowers OAKLEY into the prone position. The strobe effect stops.)

MASON
(MASON kneels.)
You had to find yourself.
(MASON runs a hand over OAKLEY'S eyes, closing them.)

OAKLEY
(Lights go down as a spot rise on OAKLEY'S Body.)
You left me for California. I couldn't compete with an entire state. I thought you'd come back. I'm returning to the smell and softness of the moist earth in that hollow tree. Skin and hair. Bodies pressed in detritus. The memory of earth rot... of dirt in my fingernails can't rewrite this ending. The pain seems distant. Irrelevant. Nothing more.

MASON
Dear Skylar,
What were you feeling when my life slipped away?

(BLACKOUT)
(END)

Screenplay

EPITAPH

NOTICE: This screenplay deals with sensitive material. If you are in crisis, DIAL 988. The 988 Lifeline is a national network of local crisis centers that provides free and confidential emotional support to people in suicidal crisis or emotional distress 24 hours a day, 7 days a week in the United States.

INT. STUDIO APARTMENT – NIGHT

There is a window and the only door is open. Simple furnishings. A futon-type bed. A vase of dead flowers sits on the dresser.

OAKLEY, in gray sweats, sits slumped in a semi-lotus position, head bowed. DEAD. Oakley's long hair covers the face. Hands stretch out, palms up. A razor blade rests against the left middle finger. The right wrist exposed and dark from blood.

Next to Oakley's left hand is a homemade, wooden frame holding a photo.

INSERT - THE PICTURE FRAME

Wood burned in the frame, "To Oakley, Love Skyler." It's fingerprinted in blood. In the picture, Oakley leans in to a similarly aged SKYLAR in a forest. Their arms are crossed. Expressions of mock indifference.

BACK IN STUDIO APARTMENT

Oakley wears earbuds. A cell phone lies nearby. Detective MASON, in a black suit (no tie), wears surgical gloves and stands near Oakley.

Mason kneels, gently moving Oakley's hair away to press gloved fingers to Oakley's carotid.

              MASON
What were you feeling when your life
slipped away?

Mason removes an ear bud from Oakley's ear, holding it near his ear. He sets it down by the cell phone and picks up the phone. Tapping the screen, he peruses it and sets it down.

     MASON (CONT'D)
"River." Playing in a loop? Why Joni Mitchell? Why "River"?

Mason picks up the picture, considers it briefly, and places it down before standing and stepping to the bed to pick up a sheet of paper.

     OAKLEY
   (not moving, loud)
Isn't it obvious?

     MASON
It's never obvious. Never one hundred percent.

     OAKLEY
   (lifts head)
I loved to dance. He loved to dance. We were nymphs. We danced in open fields... in the woods... in the rivers... I loved music. It beat back the voices in my head... but sometimes it haunted me. Then the music ended.

     MASON
An eternity of nothingness-

     OAKLEY
   (flip of the hand)
"...a brief strut upon the stage," and then an eternity of nothingness.

Mason crosses to the dresser and touches the dead flowers.

CUTAWAY - HOLLOWED OUT TREE TRUNK IN A FOREST

Oakley's left hand is pressed against the tree. It's joined by Skylar's right hand, which touches Oakley's pinky to pinky before sliding over with fingers clasping.

> OAKLEY (V.O.)
> I loved him. When he came to me that first night, I wasn't ready. He rested his head on my shoulder. I thought he just wanted to be held, but he hungered for something that brought thunder. And joy.

BACK IN STUDIO APARTMENT

Mason returns to Oakley.

> OAKLEY
> I thought I liked girls, but the way he was touching me felt-- eternally familiar. Skyler made me crazy.

Oakley's head drops. COP enters.

> COP
> Detective? M.E.'s on the way. Suicide?

> MASON
> Sometimes, I feel like I understand it.

> COP
> Just another dumb kid who didn't value life.

Cop moves to the dresser, checking drawers. Oakley's head pops up.

                    MASON
          Officer, move away from the dresser. This is
          still a crime scene.

                    OAKLEY
          I'm actually fucking here, you know.

                    COP
          It's a waste of air. These people are better
          off in the ground, anyway.

                    OAKLEY
          YOU. DON'T. KNOW. ME.

                    MASON
          Don't be crass. We don't know enough.

                    OAKLEY
          Fuck you both. I loved life. And dancing.
          And music. …and coffee.

                    COP
          Is there anything in the note?

                    MASON
          Hints. There are always hints.

                    COP
                    (sarcastic)
          Poor kid, right?

> MASON
> (to self)
> There seems to be some sexual ambiguity.

> COP
> Ah. There it is. That's what's wrong with this country. Christ! God gives us everything we need. What's wrong with the kids these days? They've got everything they need. They have it too easy.

Mason's attention snaps back to COP.

CUTAWAY - HOLLOWED OUT TREE TRUNK IN A FOREST

Skylar stands naked in front of the tree. He crouches, climbing into the hollowed-out tree.

BACK IN STUDIO APARTMENT

> OAKLEY
> Why should you care? What do you know about anything? What do you know about me? Asshat! You're a fucking cliché. Just like me, cosmic space will feed on your face. God is dead, and we're next.

> MASON
> Officer. Please wait outside.

> COP
> I'm just saying that you only need to look between your legs to know who you are.

MASON
Bring the M.E. when they arrive.

Cop exits in a bit of a huff.

OAKLEY
M.E.? What do we need the Medical Examiner for?
(beat)
M.E.. Me.

MASON
Was this really a suicide?

OAKLEY
Duh!

MASON
Good looking kid.

OAKLEY
I've been told.

MASON
(reading note)
"Dear Skylar." Not, "Dear World." Is this murder? Nah.

OAKLEY
I miss Skylar. I haven't seen him since he left me. It seems an eternity of aching. I only have the picture now. I can't remember his smell, his touch. It's just a fantasy now. We won't meet on some greater plane of existence. Will we?

MASON
(Picks up the photograph.)
Is this your Skylar?

OAKLEY
Of course it's him. He loved me for who I am. For a while anyway.

MASON
Was it that hard?

OAKLEY
Harder than you can imagine.

MASON
To not know who you are? To not be allowed to be who you are?

CUTAWAY - HOLLOWED OUT TREE TRUNK IN A FOREST

Skylar reaches out with a hand. Naked, Oakley takes the hand and climbs into the hollow with Skylar.

BACK IN STUDIO APARTMENT

OAKLEY
Maybe it was love through suffering. Or maybe just living through suffering and the love was secondary. Why do words fail me? No one heard me when I cried. No one in the angelic orders. No one from the court of God. Skylar stopped pressing me against his heart.

MASON
Just this picture, and a lonely cry in a note to Skylar.

OAKLEY
Is that all it is, detective? Just a greater angel making time stand still in a moment that I thought was forbidden. My time with time has passed.

MASON
Why is your entire existence reduced to this picture and a lonely cry in a note to someone named, Skylar?

OAKLEY
Skylar was my biggest regret, because I fell in love with him. Oh, he made me laugh so hard that I peed myself. Our moment... our moment...

MASON
You're gay?

OAKLEY
(exasperated sigh)
I'm ambiguous. This is my interpreted world... my requiem... I'm gone now.

MASON
But it really doesn't matter anymore, because you're dead.

OAKLEY
You all are.
(beat)

OAKLEY (CONT'D)
Will I smell like the wet autumn leaves,
rotting on the ground?

Mason places the picture next to OAKLEY and kneels to pull and tie OAKLEY's hair into a pony tail.

MASON
I'm so sorry. "...a brief strut upon the stage,"
and then an eternity of nothingness.

Oakley and Mason stand and the two morph into each other exchanging places and clothing.

COP (O.S.)
This way. The detective's waiting for you.

MEDICAL EXAMINER (O.S.)
I can find my way.

COP (O.S.)
Nothing for me to do out here, and she's
kinda dodgy. If you catch my meaning.

MEDICAL EXAMINER (O.S.)
I'm sure I'll be able to sort it all out.

COP (O.S.)
Sure. Whatever.

Mason and Oakley have changed clothing and places. Mason no longer wears the surgical gloves. Oakley wears them. Oakley lowers Mason into the semi-lotus position that Oakley previously occupied.

Enter MEDICAL EXAMINER, wearing surgical gloves, carrying a camera and small supply case. Cop follows and stands looking out of the window.

Oakley puts the ear bud in MASON's ear and stands to face—

> MEDICAL EXAMINER
> What do you have, detective?

With deft efficiency, Medical Examiner photographs different angles of the body. The razor. The phone.

> OAKLEY
> Apparent suicide. Unrequited love. Trans identity issues. Take your pick--another lost soul. Left a note.

> MEDICAL EXAMINER
> All in the note?

> OAKLEY
> Mostly.

> MEDICAL EXAMINER
> Ambiguity can be painful, I'm sure. Interesting. If you look along his arm, you can see where he's a cutter. Suicide is rarely the motive behind cutting. The cause of death is a different kind of cut. From the wound, not a murder, I'm sure.

Medical Examiner bags the razor and the phone--scans the note.

> OAKLEY
> (picks up the photo)
> I believe they're together in this picture. I'll have to run him down, but I don't think it will lead anywhere. Just unrequited love.

Hands the photo to the Medical Examiner.

> MEDICAL EXAMINER
> Idyllic. Like a place that I'd want to be. Pictures are worth a thousand words.

> OAKLEY
> Pictures can be deceiving.

> MASON
> It feels… familiar.

> COP
> D.B.'s ride is here. Are you ready to bag 'em?

Medical Examiner bags the photo, placing it in his box.

> MEDICAL EXAMINER
> In a moment.
> (to Oakley)
> Help me stretch him flat. Any family?

Oakley and Medical Examiner pull Mason from his lotus position, stretching him prone.

> OAKLEY
> None so far.

Medical Examiner lifts the waist band of the sweats to confirm.

>   MEDICAL EXAMINER
>   May be Trans, but the organs are male.

>   COP
>   What'd I tell you, detective. Just check
>   between the legs.

>   MEDICAL EXAMINER   OAKLEY
> Take it outside.   Take it outside.

>   MEDICAL EXAMINER (CONT'D)
>   Have them bring in the gurney.

>   COP
>   I'll send 'em up. You can escort the body
>   out; I'm going off shift.
>   (exit Cop)

>   MASON
>   (prone, looking up at Oakley
>   in the suit)
>   Not even one final plea? It's strange. No
>   longer inhabiting the earth. I felt the world
>   inside me just then.

Medical Examiner collects gear and walks to the door. Exit Medical Examiner.

>   OAKLEY
>   (standing, looking down on
>   Mason in the sweats)
>   Skylar? Do you remember the time that you
>   climbed into a huge hollowed out tree? You

> OAKLEY (CONT'D)
> were in all of your glory. You told me that
> you'd never done it in a tree before.

CUTAWAY - HOLLOWED OUT TREE TRUNK IN A FOREST

Skylar and Oakley are entwined in an embrace, unmoving. Oakley's fingers probe the dirt.

> OAKLEY (V.O.)
> I remember melding into that soft, moist
> earth. With you. Into you. The millipedes
> fled from our embrace.

BACK IN STUDIO APARTMENT

> MASON
> (prone, looking up at Oakley
> in the suit)
> We played in a world of worlds. You had to
> find yourself, and you left me for California.
> I couldn't compete with an entire state.

> OAKLEY
> (standing, looking down on
> Mason in the sweats)
> I thought you'd come back.
> (kneeling face-to-face with
> Mason in the sweats)
> I'm returning to the smell and softness of the
> moist earth in that hollow tree.

Mason, still prone, wears the suit.

> OAKLEY (CONT'D)
> Skin and hair. Bodies pressed in detritus. The memory of earth rot... of dirt in my fingernails can't rewrite this ending.

Oakley, in sweats, looks down on Mason.

> OAKLEY (CONT'D)
> The pain seems distant. Irrelevant. Nothing more.

Mason, in suit, stands over and looks down on Oakley in sweats. He kneels and runs a hand over Oakley's eyes, closing them.

CUTAWAY - HOLLOWED OUT TREE TRUNK IN A FOREST

Skylar and Oakley are entwined. Oakley's hand reaches into the dirt, digging. Grasping. Then still.

> MASON (V.O.)
> "Dear Skylar, What were you feeling when my life slipped away?"

<u>END</u>

Mini-Epic Poem

PACIFIC THEATER

(Winner of the 2017 Maryland State Arts Council
Individual Artist Award based solely on Artistic Merit)

I.

My Darling Baby

These are the days that will live in infamy, when
Children play war with penknives and letter openers

    fall on them

Piercing small hearts
Pumping their bodies dry.

Grownups collect the knives of the house to destroy them
    impotent because the house needs knives

that cut bodies down
like the Springfield loading clip -- unspent
hidden among the South Pacific seashells in my Gray Box

We are Christian warriors that swell in the populism
behind our banners and unrelenting barbarism

My warrior's patch, locked away -- waiting for a century
of being reasonable that does not come

As we slip into the shades of night…
The Gray Box surfaces into the light

and opens another darkness deep in the unclean river of

    Strength for Service
        to
    God and Country.

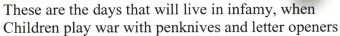

II.

Dearest

I am not the Gray Box.

It does not define me in
    four, by
      nine and three quarters, by
        eight and three quarters
            inches

Bound and stained by rust, cum, blood and salt water

    Awash in the fire and oil of screaming sailors
    and sinking ships
The Gray Box was created for me
    issued to me
    like so many other gray boxes
    long tumbled into time.

I am not the Gray Box.

The handle and latch are still solid,
    weathering decade upon decades, until

The box confronts me, and

If I release the latch
    I will have to remember

An awkward embrace with Pandora.

III.

My Darling

I am not the Gray Box.

The tiny cowries have settled to the bottom
with live rounds that I wish I had forgotten

A simple memory midst the simple drive to kill.

    Cowries.
    Roll in soft surf.
    Oblivious to the bittersweet call
    I collect them like a child.

    sweet

    Kill them All.
        Obliterate Them.

My secret code hides under these shells.

    My Darling - South China
    Dearest - North China
    Carol Dear - Hawaii
    My Own - Philippines
    Hi Honey - Australia
    Hello Darling - Japan
    My Sweet - On Board Ship
    Dearest Love - Some South Pacific Isle
    My Darling Baby - On My Way to the States or
    Soon to Leave for States
    Sweetest - Samoa
    Dearest Carol - I Don't Know

IV.

Dearest Love

Things you must not know.

I walk into the tent I share with men-of-war.

> Cork and Donny fuck on Cork's bunk.
>> My legs suck a breath, and I slip away.

Blood rushing unbridled

I flee

The sun coats me all the way to the beach --

> -- where men bathe naked in the sun and surf, unaware.

Compounding the noise in my head

Laugh and snap pictures of each other
> keep their hands cupped over

> -- the jetty extension from the shore to trap shifting sands.

I watch and lust after each lick of the wave on the stones, on my

> flesh

Drive me toward my rifle to pierce and rip flesh in response.

V.

Carol Dear

Donny died. You remember him
         hanging with Cork along
         San Francisco Bay
Before Cork professed his love to you

Friendly fire, they say
         Cracked, crimson teeth.

Donny saved me from a daydream
         just the other day
Knocking me from the rat-tat-tat-tat of a stray Zero

I never told him

The Men 'showed' him to keep him from leaving a hospital bed.

Fighting different wars.
         Cork is broken -- he doesn't know about us.

His love confuses me, but

It's Christmas

We share the ho-ho-ho with half undressed native women dancing with Santa --

This is all they had for us before we ship out.

I put all this in the Gray Box of memories.

Happy Christmas.

VI.

Sweetest

Everyday it's a new one -- this time Conti went down in a bomber flight between L.A. and Lowry Field.

Not even a good warrior's death

Here, doctors try to heal the dark diseases of
      resigned natives with deformed limbs and penises
that droop like giant burls of pin oak bark.

The elephant disease hangs from biceps,
      dripping from thighs and groins

Even babies

Medicine Men hover over infected flesh
beat it softly with bamboo
      in a mindful trance

The pictures of this different war are tucked away in the Gray Box.

Photographs of circus show freaks and naked warriors.
      and I can't take my eyes away. Nude men.

Naked men with guns.

and hard visage --

What am I?

VII.

Dearest Carol

We make our bunks the same way -- every day

    Attention
to detail
             drum, drum, drum
Always ready --

    Jack Benny came
    brought his show to our outpost.

They took my picture with us standing
    next to Cork's bunk

All I can see is Donny and Cork fucking
    slapping against Jack's pant leg

I like Jack
    and want to fly away with him, but

I am on an overland patrol

    where we find two half-baked Japs
    slumbering in a halftrack.

Mummified by the hot and salt

No one has come for them

Predators passing by
    pausing to sniff

Will we be prey or alive to cheer to Jack's pretty girls?

VIII.

My Sweet

Ozone air.

    A thousand ships slice the waves.

ROI NAMUR -- 1944

A giant moving machine sweeps fear in the hearts of our enemy

They want to go home
    but worship an emperor.

    Cork shipped out with secret orders

I wanted him --

    -- but penned a letter telling him that we married on my last leave --

I last saw him with Izzy --
    the two slipping off for a shower.

Write him
    Tell him God ordained us.

My memory of Donny and all this slides away --

    If I could have felt him

Inside me, maybe it -- this war would have been different.

He is inside my Gray Box.

IX.

My Darling Baby

I am not the Gray Box.

It does not define me.

    A great cloud in 1945 saved us from the final battle.

I am told.

We parted ways,

    among letters and promises to always connect.

But I left the memories of war,

    not to be defined by naked fellows, mummy corpses and Exit signs.

The letters and photos and Springfield rounds and naked men are secure --

    -- when the latch is closed

On the final bit of me, now dust.

I am not the Gray Box --

    which is set upon the pyre of lost opportunities.

"I learned this, at least, by my experiment; that if one advances confidently in the direction of his dreams, and endeavors to live the life which he has imagined, he will meet with a success unexpected in common hours."
— Henry David Thoreau, *Walden*

"There's more beauty in truth, even if it is dreadful beauty."
— John Steinbeck, *East of Eden*

"The Beats and the Pranksters showed us different ways of opting out of society. They were both the personification of countercultural movements. The Beats were trying to change literature, and the Pranksters were trying to change the people and the country. Kesey, in fact, was his own cultural revolution, striving to keep the upbeat, freedom-loving spirit of America alive."
— Sterling Lord, *Lord of Publishing: A Memoir*

"If you ever get down about humanity, and there are often so many reasons to do so, think about the people in your life and strangers that would help you given the chance. Think about all the people you've never met that you've helped through one means or another. That should give you a little hope."
— Bruce F. Press

Acknowledgements

My love and thanks to my family,

> My spouse, Ann, who has encouraged my writing across decades of work, always being honest in her appraisals, even crying at the sad parts. She has touched every part of this manuscript.
>
> Mom and Dad, who paid for typing my first full-length novel manuscript in 1976. Their belief never wavered.
>
> My son Sean, a key editor on this manuscript and a first reader. My daughter, Amy, who worked on design elements for this project. My son William, for his business acumen and giving me the fuel to finish this project. All of you have kept my spirit strong in my creative enterprises, especially in my dark times.
>
> My sisters and brothers, Bill, Becci (a first reader), Mary, Dave and Jean, who have championed all of my creative efforts. Rest in Peace, Davey.

My love and thanks to my friends,

> Gabe Fremuth who is a stalwart in my writing life. Gabe is a brainstorming consultant and first reader, as well as a co-author on other projects. I can't imagine my writing life without your thoughtful and perceptive input. At one time, Gabe was a student. Today, he is a mentor.

Sam LeGrys, who, like Gabe, was a student, now turned mentor. Sam's unflagging generosity of spirit gives me strength and hope.

Julie Press, for being who you are—a reader, critic, and cheerleader. Thanks for being true and supportive of my creative enterprises.

Ben and Mary Somerville, who have always been anchors, mentors, and spiritual advisors. Always in my head. I love you both!

My thanks and gratitude to the graduate faculty of Johns Hopkins University's AAP Writing Program, especially my thesis advisor, Elly Williams, who inspired me to draft both short stories contained herein.

My life and my work have always been an archipelago—islands that are separate and yet connected, in my case, spiritually, and intellectually. I thank my editor, Dr. Diana Hume George, for guiding me to that title and for her patience, grace, enthusiasm, and expertise in honing and polishing my manuscript. From her, I learned new ways to see, hear, and touch the words that have formed so much of my existence.

This book project was made possible in part by the Maryland State Arts Council (MSAC), and I am eternally grateful for their generous support. To discover more about the MSAC and how they impact Maryland, visit MSAC.org.

The author appreciates the Sponsors of the 100-Free-Books-Giveaway:
>Peggi Stallings Gregory
>William & Lauren Gossard
>Ann & James Gossard
>Jeffrey Burt

The author is grateful to the Donors of the 100-Free-Books-Giveaway:
- Amy Gossard
- Benjamin Charles Press
- Ed Nadeau
- Jeanne Busch
- Monica Lee Bellais
- Robert Kanner
- Steve & Barbara Tessier
- Becci Kuligowski
- Brian & Kathleen Gregory
- James T. Galbreath
- Ken Mays
- Paul Bayne
- Ronald C. Spinosa
- Thomas J. Burke

The author thanks all of the Story Backers of the 100-Free-Books-Giveaway.

Bio

James Gossard is an award-winning Maryland film director/producer and writer. His work represented in *Archipelago* includes plays, poetry, screenwriting, and fiction. His latest film project, *Divine Instinct*, is a feature-length, award-winning documentary about recluse sculptor Gary Spinosa.

In the past, he worked as a freelance journalist in Montana, writing for wildlife journals. StoryPros named his screenplay White Dust in its Top-Ten Action-Thrillers. His screenplays have been optioned and earned laurels in the *DC Spotlight on Screenwriters*. His stage plays have been produced and received awards, including the Maryland State Arts Council (MSAC) Individual Artist Award for his script *September Moon*. His poetry received the highest MSAC Individual Artist Award.

After studying creative writing at the University of Montana, he received his M.A. in Writing from Johns Hopkins University. A member of DC Women in Film & Video, he has taught screenwriting at Howard Community College and other venues. His current project is a science fiction novel *A Dangerous Species*. He lives with his spouse, Ann, in Ellicott City, Maryland.